Maria Sibylla Merian
NEW BOOK OF FLOWERS

Maria Sibylla Merian

NEW BOOK OF FLOWERS

With an Epilogue by Thomas Bürger

PRESTEL

Munich · London · New York

Print of the colour plates taken from:
Maria Sibylla Merian's *Neues Blumenbuch*, Nuremberg, 1680.
Reproduced from the original edition kept in the Sächsische
Landesbibliothek – Staats- und Universitätsbibliothek Dres-
den.

Plates 2 and 3 have been reproduced by kind permission
from the original edition in the Landesamt für Denkmalpflege Sachsen.

Cover design showing plate 6 (Tulip "Diana", Tulip "Veue")

Translated from the German by Michael Ashdown
Edited by Christopher Wynne

© Prestel Verlag,
Munich · London · New York, 1999

Library of Congress Catalog Card Number: 99-62668

Prestel Verlag
Mandlstraße 26, D-80802 Munich · Germany
Tel.: (+49 89) 381709-0; Fax: (+49 89) 381709-35;
West 22nd Street, New York, NY 10010, USA
Tel.: (212) 627-8199; Fax (212) 627-9866;
4 Bloomsbury Place, London WC1A 2QA
Tel.: (0171) 3235004, Fax (0171) 6368004

Prestel books are available worldwide.
Please contact your nearest bookseller or write to one of
the above adresses for information concerning your local
distributor.

Designed by Maja Thorn
Lithography by LVD, Berlin
Printed by Passavia-Druckerei, Passau
Bound by Kunst- und Verlagsbuchbinderei, Leipzig

Printed in Germany on acid-free paper

ISBN 3-7913-2080-7

Vorrede

an den

Natur- und Kunst-liebenden Leser:

Er Glorwürdigste Keyser / Maximilian / sahe (a) einsmals / auf der Reise / einen alten Bauren Stämme setzen und impfen; den ließ Er vor sich kommen / und fragte / was für Früchte er da pflantze? Der Bauer sagte / er setze Dattelbäume. Der Keyser lachte / und sprach: Ey Bäuerlein / die Datteln tragen erst in hundert Jahren Früchte; das wirst du nicht erleben / daß du davon issest! Der Bauer antwortete: Ja / Gnädiger Herr / ich weiß es wohl; ich thue es aber GOtt zu Ehren / und den Nachkommen zu Nutz! Diese Rede und That gefiel dem Keyser so wol / daß Er dem Mann hundert Gülden schenken ließ / Also ward ihm seine Sorg und Arbeit für die Nachkommen reichlich belohnet / ob er gleich der gepflantzten Bäume Früchte nicht genoß. Hingegen diejenige / welche entweder Blumen ziehen / oder verschenken / sind weder auf GOtt / noch ihre Nachkommen groß bedacht; sondern hätten gern lieber heut / dann morgen / ihren Nutzen / den sie dadurch suchen. Vom theuren Blumenkauff schreibt Neterranus / (b) daß vom Jahr 1633. bis 37. in einer Holländischen Stadt über eine Million Goldes verhandelt worden. Eine Blume / von den Tulpenhändlern Semper Augustus genant / habe man für 2000. Niederländische Gülden verkaufft; welche ums Jahr 1637. für kein Geld mehr zu kauffen gewesen / dieweil derer nur zwo / eine zu Amsterdam / die andere zu Harlem / vorhanden waren. Man sagte auch / daß einer einen Garten von Tulipanen gehabt / für welchen / samt den Blumen / ihm 70000. Gülden wären angeboten worden; er aber habe die nicht annehmen / sondern seinen Garten / mit den Blumen / behalten wollen. Auf diesen (c) Handel / weil er anfangs so wol trug / begaben sich die Leute so gar / daß die Weber ihre Stühle zu Geld gemacht / und an die Blumen gelegt; Ihrer viel haben schöne / köstliche Häuser / Landgüter / und alles / was sie gehabt / verkaufft / auch grosse / auf Zinß ausgeliehene Geldsummen wiederum eingezogen / und auf solche Blumen gewagt / die weder Geruch noch Geschmack hatten; nur daß sie mit einer flüchtigen Augenweide lüsterne Hertzen eine kurtze Zeit ergötzten. Als im Jahr 1679. den 12. Novemb. der jetzige Papst die Milaneser-Kirche S. Carlo besichtiget / und Ihm auf dem Rückweg einige Blumen verehret wurden; legte Er in diejenige Schüssel / darinnen man solche überreicht / einen Brief von etlich tausend Cronen; bey der Kammer solche zu empfangen.

So viel vermag nemlich die Natur / mit ihrer holdseligen Zierde / bey grossen Liebhabern auszurichten / daß sie die Beschauung solcher Blumen höher / als ihrer Schätze achten / und lieber ihren Reichthum / dann ihre Lust vermindern wollen. Um welcher willen sie vielleicht desto weniger zu verdenken / indem so bunte Meisterstücke die heimliche Neigung an sich habe / daß sie diejenigen nicht so wol mit sehenden Augen blind / als mit blinden Augen sehend machen: Zumal so wie der Sineser (d) Blumenkönig /

(a) Casp. Titius in Loc. Theol. pag. 635. (b) Meteran. lib. 51. (c) Mart. Grundmann / in der Geschicht Schul / Bl. 175. (d) Joh. Neuhoff in Beschreibung Sina / Cap. XV. Bl. 327. 328.

König / Meutang genant / nur in unsrem Sinn beschauen / dessen grosse Blätter / weißlicht / und mit Purpur vermengt; wiewol auch etliche gantz roth / und gantz gelb gefunden werden. Die Sinesische Rose mag billich eine Wunderblume darum heissen / dieweil sie ihre Farb täglich zweymal verändert; indem sie bald Purpurfarb / bald Schneeweiß ist. Zu geschweigen der auch Schneeweissen / und auf kleinen Bäumlein wachsenden Mogorin / welche der Blume Jesamin nicht unähnlich; ohne daß sie mehr Blätter / dazu auch einen viel edlern Geruch hat / womit eine eintzige Blum ein gantzes Haus erfüllen kan. Wiewol Europa nicht das geringste Asien hierinnen bevor gibt; sintemal der Chur-Pfältzische Lustgarten aus Engelland dermassen bereichert und gezieret worden / daß allda beedes Scharlachfarbe und blaue Jesamin / schattirte Rosen von allerhand Farben / schwartze Johannisbäre / die den Wachholdern dem Geschmack nach wol gleichen / rothe Stichelbäre / nebenst vielen andern seltenen Denckwürdigkeiten / mit höchster Verwunderung / gesehen werden: Als an einem solchen Ort / woselbst Apollo Hof hält / und alle schöne Wissenschafften mehr dann Fürstlich begnadet werden. Es läst sich auch nicht verschweigen / was der wegen seiner vortrefflichen Schrifften hochberühmte / und ungemeiner Freundlichkeit volbeliebte Mann / P. Bohusl. Balbinus (e) unlängst von Böhmerland glaubwürdig berichtet / wie nemlich die Angelica / auf dem Riesengebürg / höher dann ein Mensch / und dicker dann ein Arm / abgebrochen worden.

Dieweil nun aber / eben in dieser Blüe- und Blumenreichen Frühlingszeit / die Kunst von der Natur / als zu einem freywilligen und anmuthigen Zweykampff / gleichsam ausgefordert wird; so hat man nicht ermangeln wollen noch sollen / diesem nach wiewol schwachem jedoch willigem Vermögen / einige Vergnügung zu leisten: Und dannenhero diß neue Blumenbuch nicht um eigenes Nutzens willen (wie von jenen beschehen) sondern vielmehr der Lobgierigen Jugend zum besten / und dann auch der künfftigen Nachwelt zum Andenken / an das Liecht stellen wollen: Damit solches so wol zum Nachreissen und Mahlen / als dem Frauenzimmer zum Nähen / und allen Kunstverständigen Liebhabern zu Nutz und Lust dienstlich seyn möchte. Des zuversichtlichen Vertrauens / dieselbigen werden solches drey-bündige Blumenbuch eben mit derjenigen Gunstgewogenheit zu bewürdigen geruhen; womit Sie das jüngsthin ausgegebene Raupenbüchlein / wegen der darinn befindlichen Blumen und Kräuter / an- und aufgenommen / ihnen merklich belieben lassen.

So muß Kunst und Natur stets mit einander ringen /
bis daß sie beederseits sich selbsten so bezwingen /
damit der Sieg besteh' auf gleichen Strich und Streich:
So muß Kunst und Natur sich hertzen und umfangen /
und diese beederseits die Hand einander langen:
Wol dem / der also kämpft! dieweil / auf solchen Streit /
wann alles ist gethan / folgt die Zufriedenheit.

(e) Balbin. lib. 1. Miscell. Hist. R. Bohem. cap. 6. §. 5.

Regi-

Register

Des ersten Blumentheils.

Des zweyten Blumentheils.

Des dritten Blumentheils.

4. Weiß

Preamble and Table of Contents from the original edition of Maria Sibylla Merian's publication

Introductory Note

More than three centuries after it was first published, Maria Sibylla Merian's *New Book of Flowers* is still one of the most stunning collections of floral engravings in existence, remarkable for its scientific accuracy, brilliant colours, and delicate beauty.

Merian abandoned traditional modes of illustration known in 16th- and 17th-century botanical treatises for more comprehensive, balanced compositions. Combining botanic accuracy with high artistic quality, she moved away from single illustrations and, instead, fused tulips, peonies, and lilies into a cacophony of colour and detail. Merian meticulously recorded the beauty of these flowers, often emphasizing their relationship to their natural surroundings by including butterflies, caterpillars, and other insects in the work. Her copper engravings show flora and fauna inter-woven with each other, displaying the artist's love of and deep respect for nature. The careful colouring added extra charm to the prints – even today, her images of flowers and insects seem fresh and their colours radiant.

The *Book of Flowers*, published in three volumes between 1675 and 1680, was originally meant as a model and exercise book for Merian's painting classes. Soon it was recognized as one of the finest books of flower engravings. Merian went on to conduct scientific studies on insects, capturing the exotic flora and fauna of South America during a two-year stay in the Dutch colony of Surinam. With these drawings she found recognition worldwide and she is greatly admired to this day as an extraordinary artist and an independent woman.

M. S. Gräffin
M. Merians des Altern seel: Tochter.
Neues
Blumen Buch
Allen Kunstverständiger
Liebhabern zu Lust, nutz und Dienst,
mit fleiß verfertiget.
Zu finden bey
Joh. Andrea Graffen,
Mahlern in Nürnberg
im Jahr 1680.

Hyacinthus spec., *Narcissus tazetta* L.

Gefüllte Hyazinthe und
ein Stengel Tazetten

*Double Hyacinth, Bunch-
flowered Daffodil*

(No. 2)

Hyacinthus orientalis L.

Einfache blaue Hyazinthe

Common Garden Hyacinth

(No. 3)

3

Narcissus pseudonarcissus L.

Zwei einfache Narzissen

Common Daffodil

(No. 4)

4

Narcissus tazetta L.

Große orientalische Narzisse
(Tazett-Narzisse)

Bunch-flowered Daffodil

(No. 5)

5

Tulipa ›Diana‹, Tulipa ›Veue‹

Große Tulipane, Diana, samt der
kleinen, Veue, oder Wittfrau
genannt

Tulip "Diana", Tulip "Veue"

(No. 6)

6

Anemone, Fritillaria, Crocus

Anemone, Fritillari, Krokus

Anemone, Fritillary, Crocus

(No. 7)

7

Iris germanica L.

Große blaue Lilie

Bearded Iris

(No. 8)

8

Lilium pumilum DC.

Feinblättrige Lilie

Turk's Cap Lily

(No. 9)

9

Viola x *wittrockiana* Gams

Dreifaltigkeitsblümlein,
Gartenstiefmütterchen

Garden Pansy

(No. 10)

1C

Rosa ›Hollandica‹

Holländische Rose

Dutch Rose

(No. 11)

11

Paeonia

Betonien-Rose und Knopf
(Knospe)

Peony

(No. 12)

12

Der zweite Blumenteil

Second Section of Flowers

Der Titel-Blumenkranz

Garland of Flowers

(No. 1+)

FLORUM
Fasciculus Alter:
Zweyter Blumen-Theil;
so Maria Sibylla Gräffin
Matth. Merians seel: des Eltern
Tochter, nach dem Leben gemahlet
und selbst auffs Kupffer gebracht.
Zufinden in Nürnberg:
bey Joh: Andr: Graffen
Mahlern. A: 1680.

Ein Blumengehänge und
zwei Blumenkränzlein

Two Posies of Flowers and
Two Small Garlands

(No. 2+)

Primula x *pubescens* Jacq.

Schlüsselblume (Gartenaurikel)

Garden Auricula

(No. 3+)

34

Fritillaria imperialis L.

Einfache goldgelbe Kaiserkrone

Crown Imperial

(No. 4+)

4.

Tulipa ›Hevelmann‹

Schöne Tulipane (Tulpe),
der Hevelmann gen.

Tulip "Hevelmann"

(No. 5+)

'54

Erysimum cheiri (L.) Crantz

Großer gelber Veil-Stengel
(Goldlack)

Wallflower

(No. 6+)

64

Ranunculus asiaticus L.

Feuerfarbene Ranunkel

Turban (Persian) Buttercup

(No. 7+)

74

Lilium candidum L., *Galanthus nivalis* L., *Convolvulus tricolor* L.

Weiße Lilien, Schneetröpflein und blauer Bindling

Madonna Lily, Snowdrop, Dwarf Morning Glory

(No. 8+)

8ℨ

Iris

Dunkelblaue Iris oder
Schwertlilie

Iris

(No. 9+)

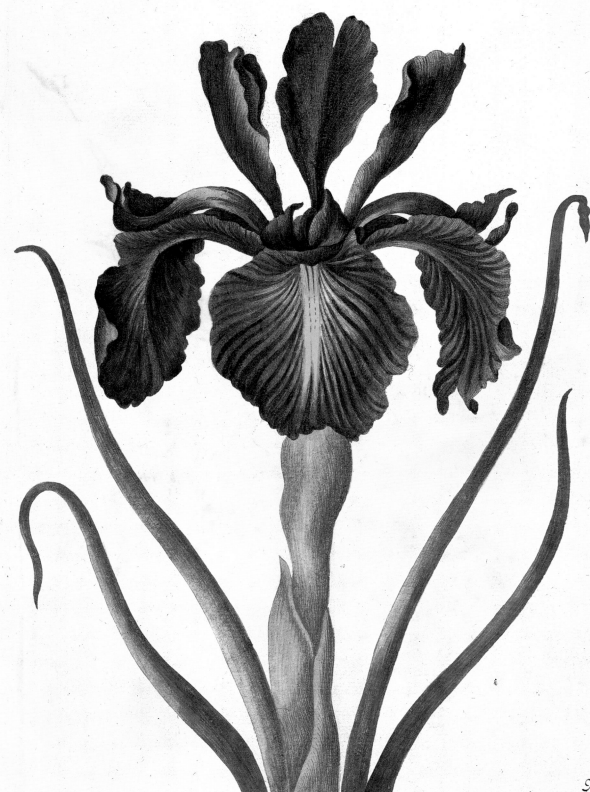

9 H

Dianthus caryophyllus L.

Negelein (Nelke),
oder Grasblumen-Stengel

Clove Pink, Carnation

(No. 10+)

104

Punica granatum L.

Granaten-Blüte

Pomegranate

(No. 11+)

Rosa gallica L., *Jasminum grandiflorum* L., *Anemone* spec.

Essigrose, weißer Jasmin, Anemone

French Rose, Jasmine, Anemone

(No. 12+)

Der dritte Blumenteil

Third Section of Flowers

Der Titel-Blumenkranz

Garland of Flowers

(No. 1–)

FLORUM
Fasciculus Tertius
Dritter Blumen-Theil:
so Maria Sibilla Gräffin
nach den Leben gemahlet,
und ins Kupffer gestochen.
Zufinden in
Nürnberg
Bey Joh: Andr: Graf-
fen Mahlern.
A° 1680.

Ein Blumen-Körblein

Small Basket of Flowers

(No. 2–)

Ein Blumen-Krüglein

Small Vase of Flowers

(No. 3–)

Erythronium dens-canis L.,
Hyacinthus orientalis L.,
Iris persica L., *Muscari* spec.

Weißer Hundszahn, rote
Hyazinthe, Iris von Persien,
Schaben-Blümlein oder Wein-
trauben-Hyazinthe

*Dog's Tooth Violet, Common
Garden Hyacinth, Persian Iris,
Grapehyacinth*

(No. 4–)

Hyacinthoides/Scilla, Tulipa
›Admiral de Moor‹, Fritillaria spec.

Blaue Stern-Hyazinthe,
Tulipane ›Admiral de Moor‹,
gefüllte Fritillarien

Bluebell or Squill, Tulip "Admiral
de Moor", Double Fritillary

(No. 5–)

5-

Anemone

Anemonen

Anemones

(No. 6–)

6

Delphinium spec., *Narcissus* spec.,
Iris latifolia (Mil.) Voss

Gefüllter Rittersporn, Josephstab,
englische Iris

Larkspur, Daffodil, Iris

(No. 7–)

7

Convallaria majalis L.,
Polianthes tuberosa L.,
Adonis annua L.

Maiblümchen, Tuberosa,
Korallenblümlein

*Lily-of-the-Valley, Tuberose,
Pheasant's Eye*

(No. 8–)

Papaver somniferum L.,
Campanula spec.

Magsamen-Blume (Mohn),
Blaues Wiesenglöcklein mit
Stieglitz oder Distelfink

Garden-Poppy, Bellflower,
with Goldfinch

(No. 9–)

9--

Capparis spinosa L., *Spartium
junceum* L.

Große Kapern-Blüte, Kunschrote

Caper, Spanish Broom

(No. 10–)

Passiflora caerulea L.

Passionsblume

Blue Passion-flower

(No. 11–)

11.

Tropaeolum majus L., *Tagetes*
spec.*; Myosotis* spec.

Kapuzinerkresse, Studentenblume; Vergiß mein nicht

Nasturtium; Marigold;
Forget-me-not

(No. 12–)

Epilogue

THOMAS BÜRGER

MARIA SIBYLLA MERIAN'S BOOK OF FLOWERS

The long tradition of the floral picture experienced a true revival in the seventeenth century. The symbolic art of Christian Europe, scientific curiosity, and, not least, the joy of the representative and the exotic or foreign, produced the finest floral still lifes of the early Modern age.[1]

Maria Sibylla Merian did not paint her floral works in oil, as did many painters of flowers from Brueghel to Picasso, whose still lifes draw a wide public into the world's museums. Instead, Merian's drawings, watercolours, and hand-coloured books – being sensitive to the effects of light – are sheltered from its direct glare, and hence can only be made accessible through publications such as this volume.

Merian's *Book of Flowers* deserves the revived interest for several reasons. Her first work is a very rare one, and, in this colouring, it is unique. Just by looking at its pages, the artist's approach to her very own subject becomes clear. The *Book of Flowers* unites different types of floral painting: in addition to decorative garlands, a basket and a vase of flowers are depicted in the tradition of still-life pictures, there are various 'floral portraits', and the first indications of Merian's new ecological perspective on the biological life cycles of flowers and insects.

For many artists, flowers and floral pictures are an inexhaustible source of inspiration for the imitation of nature and its representation in art. In the preface to her *Book of Flowers* Maria Sibylla Merian characterizes the concurrence of nature and art as a 'spontaneous and graceful duel':

> Art and nature shall always be wrestling/
> until they mutually conquer each other/
> so that the victory is on the same stroke and line:
> that which is conquered, conquers at the same
> time![2]

Art seeks to surpass nature, and yet is repeatedly overwhelmed by the beauties of the natural world. This great and perpetually new contest between self-assertion and modesty is also the theme of the artist and scientist Maria Sibylla Merian. She places her œuvre at the service of nature by making us aware of the miniature natural works of art in her pictures of flowers, butterflies and caterpillars. The scientific perspective distinguishes her painting from that of others, and becomes increasingly evident in the course of her œuvre, setting it apart from the many more or less dilettante artists who draw or paint floral motifs in watercolours. Moreover, it distinguishes her from those still-life artists who apparently seek to outdo nature with the high art of trompe l'œil,[3] or who, by using artistic licence, wish to confront nature, as it were, with an independent work of art.

Maria Sibylla Merian may be regarded as the first female German artist of renown. Her fame is due in equal measure to both her œuvre and her astonishing biography.

She asserted herself as an artist, although, according to the decrees of the time, still-life painting in oil and botanical illustration were the preserve of men. She left her husband, and provided single-handedly for her children. She joined the Labadists[4] to live her religiousness to the full, and yet she remained true to her own scientific thirst for knowledge. She was a cosmopolite of Old Europe, and toured South America in order to extend her own horizons as well as those of her readers. She wrote books for teaching purposes, illustrated, published and translated her own works, and was thus author, artist and publisher in one. In spite of this industriousness, she forgot or eschewed any monument to herself in the form of self-portraits or autobiographical notes. Hence, it remained, and still remains to this day, for the admirer of her œuvre to describe, research and relate her life's story.

Maria Sibylla Merian was born on April 4, 1647, in Frankfurt am Main, and died on January 13, 1717, in Amsterdam. She spent the greater span of her seventy years in these two cities. During the time of the wars of religion in Europe, Frankfurt had granted the admission of many Dutch refugees, and, with their aid, had established itself as a financial centre. Owing to its neutrality, the Free City of the Reich, in which the German Kaisers had been proclaimed and crowned for decades, was spared destruction during the Thirty Years' War, although not spared the plague. Merian spent the first twenty-three years of her life in this city of commerce and book fairs, until she followed her husband to Nuremberg in 1670. Nuremberg's second cultural revival after the time of Dürer was intimately connected with the flourishing book and publishing sector. She spent eleven years in this city, and it was here, between 1675 and 1680, that her three-part *Book of Flowers* was published.

For the last twenty-six years of her life Maria Sibylla lived in Amsterdam, a period interrupted only by her two-year journey to Surinam, South America (1699-1701). With the rise of Dutch sea power and the associated flourish in colonial trade, Amsterdam became the prime commercial city in northern Europe. The three commercial and artistic centres, namely Frankfurt am Main, Nuremberg and Amsterdam chiefly influenced Merian's creative environment. All three were influential printing and publishing centres, and were also major cities of the European book trade in which the Merian family had a good name as a publisher of books and engravings.

Maria Sibylla hardly knew her father, Matthäus the Elder, the most famous member of the Merian family. He died in 1650, just three years after her birth. His works of graphic art and the books that he published could compare, like few others of war-impoverished Germany, with representative documents of the best printing works in France, England or the Netherlands.

To this day, the name of Matthäus Merian the Elder is associated with exquisitely detailed views of cities, with which he gradually replaced the outdated, schematic pictures of such works as Schedel's *World Chronicle*. Thanks to his views of German cities prior to the destruction since the Thirty Years' War we have

an indispensable record to this day. Merian had also helped initiate the *Theatrum Europaeum*, a unique chronicle of the Thirty Years' War. The first five folio volumes were published during his lifetime, and by 1738, his heirs had completed the work – twenty-one volumes in all with a total of 1,432 illustrations.

In the *Book of Flowers*, and in her later works, the author and artist Maria Sibylla proudly named herself "M. Merians des Aeltern seel. Tochter" ("the late M. Merian the Elder's daughter"). Her father's first marriage was to the daughter of the successful Oppenheim publisher and copperplate engraver Johann Theodor de Bry, whose father, Theodor de Bry, had been forced to leave the Netherlands in 1570 on account of his religious beliefs. After the death of his father-in-law in 1624, Merian took over the business and moved to Frankfurt. There, he acquired citizenship in 1626, after having first renounced that of Basle. There were eight children by the first marriage, including the portraitist Matthäus the Younger, and the copperplate engraver and co-partner of the publishers, Caspar Merian. A year after the death of his first wife in 1645 Merian married Johanna Sibylla Heim. Maria Sibylla was born in 1647.

The early death of the father had disastrous consequences for the large family. The eldest son, Matthäus, was forced to break off his career, and noted in his autobiography that he had "found everyone in a grieved state, while many hungry brothers and sisters were present with a stepmother, where there was only an inclination towards a good inheritance and not to a continuance of the business. Whereupon steps were taken towards division."[5] Matthäus the Younger does not speak well of the stepmother. According to him, she had used up the inheritance together with her second husband, Jacob Marrel, a "minor painter", and, after his death, was ultimately obliged to eat "the bread of charity with her daughter", Maria Sibylla.[6]

In contrast to her half-brother, Maria Sibylla was apparently very fond of her stepfather, who brought three children with him into the second marriage. Jacob Marrel (1613-1681) was a pupil of the Frankfurt still-life painter Georg Flegel, and in Utrecht he had specialized in floral still lifes. It was from him that Maria Sibylla learned the fundamentals of painting.

Whenever her stepfather was away travelling, she would go into his workshop, where the still-life painter, Abraham Mignon, and also her later husband, Johann Andreas Graff, served their apprenticeships, and may well have taught her watercolour painting, engraving and printing.

Unlike the male family members, Maria Sibylla could not travel as an apprentice. While in the early years her father worked in cities such as Zurich, Strasbourg, Nancy, Paris, Stuttgart, Augsburg, Nuremberg and Oppenheim, in addition to his native town of Basle or, while in the years of his apprenticeship, her half-brother was in Amsterdam, London, Paris or Nuremberg, amongst other places, Maria Sibylla had to rely on her domestic tuition which she received either from her mother or in the workshop. Unfortunately, we do not learn anything of Merian's artistic education from Merian herself, although we may read (in the preface to her Surinam book) that she had occupied herself with the study of insects since her youth. Later, in her study book, she recorded precisely the time and object of her first investigations. As a thirteen-year-old girl, she had observed the metamorphosis of the silk-worm, and wrote up this observation in her work journal, noting, not without pride: "I have begun this study, thank God, in Frankfurt, 1660."[7] Merian kept this journal over a period of three decades, as recorded in 1717 in St. Petersburg. For the artist and scientist Maria Sibylla Merian it was an indispensable index of works and a book of models with its watercolours and notes; for research on Merian, it is the most important manuscript and source in existence.

In 1665, the eighteen-year-old Merian married the Nuremberg painter, copperplate engraver and publisher Johann Andreas Graff (1637-1701). After having served his apprenticeship in Frankfurt and Italy, Graff had returned to the city on the River Main. The young couple lived for five years with Merian's mother in Frankfurt, and only moved to Nuremberg in 1670 with their then two-year-old daughter, Johanna Helena. Here, in his native town, the most important Upper German literary, artistic and publishing centre, Graff attempted to establish himself as an engraver and publisher in the face of great competition, but with little success. Meanwhile, his wife continued her artistic and scientific studies. In addition, there was the management of the household to attend to, as well as the education of the two children – ten years after her sister

Helena, the second daughter, Dorothea Maria, was born in 1678. Maria Sibylla gave both daughters lessons in drawing and painting, and both later showed their gratitude by assisting her.

In 1675, Joachim von Sandrart honoured the couple – with whom he was on friendly terms – in the second volume of his *Teutsche Academie*, in a short chapter with the following eloquent title: "Johann Andreas Graf/ painter/ married to Maria Sibilla Merianin, delicate painter of flowers: also sews natural and vivid flowers with the needle: etches these."[8] While Sandrart mentions Graff only in a few lines, he is all the more interested in Merian, emphasizing her famous name as well as his admiration for her dual talent, "in addition to the regulated, good management of the household,"[9] to have been so successful in painting flowers, herbs and insects. As a contemporary testimony, Sandrart's notes and appraisal are rare enough, and therefore deserve to be presented in more detail:[10]

"Johann Andreas Graf of Nuremberg … married in Frankfurt to the daughter of the renowned copperplate engraver M. Merian/ of the name of Maria Sibilla Merianin, as she was inclined from her background/ and own desire to noble painting/ as she then/ by way of this marriage/ to render the good information as demanded in the arts of drawing and painting with oils and watercolours on all sorts of decorations in flowers/ fruits and birds/ especially also in the excrements of the little worms/ flies/ gnats/ spiders and such nature of the animals/ together with their transformations/ how the same are at the beginning/ and afterwards become living animals/ together with the leaves/ whence they obtain their nourishment/ with great diligence/ grace and spirit/ both in the drawing/ and in the coloured-in colours/ and etchings accomplished in a masterly fashion/ particularly with a sort of watercolour on silken plates/ satin or other materials/ on linen, too she paints all sorts of graceful flowers and herbs/ and so that these appear in equal perfection on both sides of the linen/ and what is most remarkable/ is that such painted linen can be washed again without danger to the colours … such as these come daily to light from her expedient hands/ that she hence in this art worthy of glory/ of the natural flowers/ herbs and animals/ has the praise of being most perfect; how in the same way with silk all the above are truthfully and naturally rendered by the needle/ is most highly renowned/ how she then assists several of those/ who demand to learn and pursue such virtues/ and has drawn curious lessons/ and clearly and rationally etched them into copper ...".[11]

As a native of Nuremberg, Sandrart naturally knew that Maria Sibylla taught painting and embroidery to the daughters of respected citizens. Little is known of the colourfast fabric painting that he mentions; more however of the 'Jungfern-Companie' ('Company of Maidens', so named by Merian), to which belonged the patrician's daughter Clara Regina Imhoff, as well as women painters and daughters of famous Nuremberg copperplate engravers, such as Magdalena Fürst and Dorothea Auer. It was for these people as well as for an extended circle of self-educated acquaintances that Merian produced with her *Book of Flowers* – the first printed models and patterns "to copy and paint/ as to sew in the women's room/ and for the use and pleasure of all expert lovers of art" (Preface, 1680).

In 1679, Merian published a new book, which she had worked on for five years – parallel to her *Book of Flowers* – a work which which can be considered her main scientific work: *Wonderful transformation/ and singular flower-food of caterpillars/ wherein by a completely new invention/ the caterpillar/ worms/ butterflies/ moths/ flies/ and other such small animals/ the origin/ foods/ and transformations/ together with their time/ place and characteristics/ in the service of natural scientists/ painters/ and lovers of gardens/ are diligently studied/ concisely described/ painted from life/ engraved on copper/ and self-published ....*[12] The volume was not published in the small folio format of the *Book of Flowers*, but in the smaller quarto format. The first section of this 'Book of Caterpillars' comprises 102 pages of text and fifty illustrations.

The title page introduces the contents with Baroque eloquence. The flowers recede further into the background; as "flower-food" they remain of interest only as feed plants. Merian emphasizes the originality of her methods most effectively, proudly pointing out that she wrote, painted, engraved and published the work herself, thus producing it as author, artist and publisher in one.

This second work, too, was issued by her husband's publishing house in Nuremberg; however, it was also available in the trade-fair city of Leipzig, in order to reach a wider public. The composition of this Baroque book is typical. The title sheet – an illustrated copperplate engraving – is followed by a detailed title page, then a 'eulogy' in the form of a poem, intended as a defence against critics and to make plain the book's value. The author was Christoph Arnold (1627-1685), professor at the Egidiengymnasium and, identified by translations from English, a learned scholar. In twenty-four lines which, from a literary point of view, are modest, he compares Merian to the most learned authors of the neighbouring European countries of England, France, Italy, the Netherlands and Spain, among them Conrad Gesner, Pierre Pena and Thomas Mouffet:

> It is worthy of amazement/ that women, too,
>> dare to write / with intent/
>>> such that gives the learned assembly so much
>>>> to do.
> What Gesner/ Wotton/ Penn/ and Mufet leave/
>> to write in documents;
>>> that is what for you/ England/
>>> my Germany has now achieved/ by clever
>>>> woman's hand.[13]

The author's preface follows in three parts, first containing a formulation of modesty or humility, followed by a summary of her investigations and finally an advertising announcement of possible future continuations. For the recording of her observations, she had been urged by "learned and noble persons": "Seek therefore herein not my/ but God's honour alone/ Him/ to praise/ as a creator of also these smallest and most insignificant little worms ...".[14] The rapid switch to a presentation of her experiments and observations shows, however, that Merian did not want primarily to write an edifying text, but rather a natural history book.

Nevertheless, the exemplary fashion in which she unites religiousness and scientific urge in her work is remarkable. Pious reading in the divine book of nature and the independent search for the hidden secrets of this nature were no longer categorically mutually exclusive.

Theologians certainly continued to regard *curiositas*, scientific curiosity, with suspicion. For this reason, Merian asked Christoph Arnold to add a poem at the end of her book in order to avoid possible misunderstandings. Two of the seven verses of Arnold's *Raupen-Lied* ("Caterpillar Poem") are particularly revealing:

5.
Look at the little plants/
    with which He feeds the worms;
all flowers/ boughs and little shrubs/
    since nature shows that they/
must nourish so many thousand/
and teach us GOD'S providence:
    Look at the lowly meadow/
    And its proud purple cloak.

7.
Most beloved GOD/ so will you
    Also deal with us/ in due course of time;
Just as the caterpillars transform themselves/
    They/ who through their mortality/
again become alive/
just like the dead/ in the ground;
    Let me, poor little worm
    Be then at your command!¹⁵

No plant, no worm is so insignificant that the *providentia dei*, the providence of God for all creatures, cannot be revealed in it. According to this message in an age of fundamental scientific discoveries and deepest religiousness, the biological life cycle can, and is to be understood not only in a scientific sense, but also in a theological one. The conclusion of the poem reads like an apotheosis, and is to be expected as a matter of course by all readers who are familiar with (biblical) allegorical interpretations: every human being is a worm before God, fearful and transient, but at the same time hopeful that death will lead to a new life.

Merian wants to praise God the Creator with her representation of His creatures, but of no lesser importance, she wishes to seek out some of the still-hidden connections of the microcosm. Thus, she describes the metamorphosis of caterpillars, silkworms and maggots, how they shed their skins several times and turn into butterflies, beetles, bees and flies. For example, the tulip is now of interest as a feed plant on which – visibly brought into the foreground – she depicts the young caterpillar, the DATE STONE, "who seems to be completely dead" (pupation in its cocoon), and the "MOTH."

What is new in the book of caterpillars is not only the change of perspective from the plant to the small animals, but also the juxtaposition and concurrence of picture and text. This text/picture combination has been a classic didactic means since the Middle Ages. The mutual interpretation of picture and text is especially intimate in, for example, the lluminated manuscripts of the *Sachsenspiegel*, the most important German-language book of law from the Middle Ages to modern times. Merian uses the text to explain the temporal succession of development, which in the pictures must be depicted next to each other. She places great value on recording exactly the times she has measured, and, moreover, on describing the colours in detail, since she was only able to hand-colour a few copies herself. In order to increase the precision of the reproductions, she used an etching needle for the book of caterpillars – in addition to a burin – and, for especially delicate lines, a cold needle.

It was only through the mutual enhancement of picture and text that Merian was able to achieve a new ecological manner of representation. She did not want to list encyclopaedically and record schematically, but rather describe and illustrate the biological life cycles of the plant and animal kingdoms using the pictorial and textual possibilities open to her. In this way, she was able to attain her goal of breathing artistic life into traditional forms of representation – a new didactic balance between near-natural representation and artistic stylization.

Merian adds another note to her text on the fiftieth sheet: she described the "for some people perhaps despicable things" solely in God's honour, so that these might be: "clearer and shine forth more brightly and more splendidly among us earthly-minded people." "Otherwise I would never have let myself be talked into beginning this small but difficult work/ much less have it printed: it is odd/ when one should consider this of mine/ as a woman/ (who has to compile this in addition to her domestic duties) as an unseemly, immoderate ambition."¹⁶ With the references at the beginning and end of her work, Merian not only proved her humility and awe of God, but also wanted to defend herself against accusations of immodest ambitions and neglect of her domestic duties. At the end of her preface, she spurs herself on and gives herself courage:

The beginning is accomplished; this will now please/
so will I from now on/ practise/ in the service of
                                        the reader/
    that I retain his pleasure/ through art/
    so that one deserves praise/ and the grace
                                        of great men!¹⁷

However, before Merian could think of adding to her book of caterpillars (the second and third volumes were published with fifty illustrations each in 1683 and, posthumously, in 1717, respectively), there were several, crucial changes in her life. In 1681, her stepfather, Jacob Marrel, died. He left debts that evidently could not even be covered by the sale of the 320 remaining paintings.[18] Maria Sibylla hurried with her two daughters, then aged three and thirteen, to Frankfurt, to help her mother in her predicament. Her husband followed her only staying from time to time; her separation from him seemed to become more and more a reality during this time. However, she maintained written contact with her women friends and pupils in Nuremberg in order to lend support to her 'Company of Maidens' by giving technical and artistic advice.[19]

A further significant turning point followed in 1685. Together with her elderly mother and her two daughters, Merian joined the Labadist community in Wartha Castle in West Friesland. Jean de Labadie (1610-1674) had left the Jesuit order in 1639 and was converted to the Reformed Church in 1650. In the Netherlands, he founded a pietistic community for the pastoral revival of the official church. His main work, *La réformation de l'église par le pastorat*, had also influenced Phillip Jakob Spener, who, as a priest in Frankfurt am Main, promoted an individualistic culture of piety with private conventicles, and thus incurred the open hostility of the Lutheran orthodoxy. In 1675 – contemporaneously with Merian's *Book of Flowers* – Spener's *Pia desideria* was published, his reform programme for Lutheran pietism on the practice of piety (*praxis pietatis*) and for the revival of the church. This 'pietistic practice of piety' not only decisively inspired the development of psychological and subjective perceptions from the eighteenth century onwards, but also made contemporaries of the outgoing Baroque age more aware of a new perception of the external and internal world of experience.

It is not known what motivated the four women to join this pietistic community in West Friesland. Perhaps Merian wanted to flee the precarious financial situation following the death of her stepfather; perhaps, however, she also sought the closeness to her widowed half-brother, Caspar Merian, who had already been living in Wartha Castle since 1677. Her husband vainly hoped to win back his family by paying them a visit. The 'unconverted' was barred entry, and a drawing of the castle is all that still remains as a reminder of this visit. In 1692, Johann Andreas Graff filed for divorce in Nuremberg, pointing out that his wife had left him seven years earlier. He remarried, and died in Nuremberg in 1701.

For Merian, the failure of her marriage and her flight into a closed religious community did not mean that she simply stopped working, turning her back altogether on reality. To the contrary, she seems to have used the time to reorganise the contents of her study book, to design it calligraphically, and to expand it into a reference and model book which she could later refer to again and again. She continued her entomological research with drawings and commentaries, which indicates that her work was accepted as a practice of piety, an artistic and investigative *praxis pietatis*. Her sensibility found an appropriate outlet not in letters and autobiographical confessions – as later in the age of sentimentalism – but instead in the journal of her work.

Her life in the Labadist community remained an isolated episode. In 1688, the owner of the castle, Governor Cornelis van Aerssen, was murdered in Surinam (Dutch Guyana). In 1690, the dissolution of the community was considered. Johanna Sibylla and Maria Sibylla Merian renounced their citizenship of Frankfurt, and Merian's mother died not long after. In 1691, Maria Sibylla returned to Amsterdam with her daughters, now aged thirteen and twenty-three, as a freelance painter of flowers and insects. Here, she developed new creative strength, visiting the botanical gardens, cultivating contacts with scholars of natural history and painting marvellous watercolours which are found today in many museums throughout the world.

In 1692, her eldest daughter, Johanna Helena, married the merchant Jacob Hendrik Herolt, who, as a former member of the Labadist community, traded with the Surinam colony. Merian, now fifty-two years old, untertook the long journey to this country in the northeast of South America, where she was able to fulfil her dream of making a research expedition to examine the superabundant flora and fauna of the tropical jungle landscape. She had been able to see many exotic exhibits in Amsterdam, but now wanted to study living objects in terms of "their origin and their reproduction." Hence, she made out her will as a precautionary measure, sold her collection of pictures and specimens in February 1699, and embarked on this dangerous and costly expedition, accompanied only by her younger daughter.

Since the discovery of Surinam in 1500 by the Spanish, the colony had been under Dutch rule, despite claims from the English and French. Ownership and administration were equally divided among the West Indian Company, the City of Amsterdam, and Cornelis van Aerssen, ruler of Sommelsdijk who, as already mentioned, was later murdered by either the native inhabitants or rebelling soldiers. The African slaves who had been brought into the country cultivated sugar cane, lived under unspeakable conditions, and fled to the hinterland in large numbers before slavery was finally abolished in 1863.

Merian gives little indication of these difficult political and social conditions, or of the sanitary hardships associated with the journey. The tropical climate was a great strain on her, and she nearly died from yellow fever. She was forced to return home prematurely after two years, but she had fulfilled her dream of studying the rare flora and fauna at first hand, and bringing samples back to Europe in the form of natural specimens and preparations, as well as drawings and notes.

Maria Sibylla's ship sailed from Paramaribo, and she and her daughter arrived back in Amsterdam on September 23, 1701. Here, Merian elaborated on her observations and sketches, but also had to take on contract work to pay travel debts. She drew and painted seashells, snails and reptiles 'from life', which the merchant and natural scientist Georg Eberhard Rumpf had collected and described and which the publisher Johannes Oosterwijk now wanted to publish. Rumpf, born in Hanau near Frankfurt, was a governor on the Moluccan island of Ambon, where he died in 1702. Since the expulsion of the Portuguese and British from the Moluccas, the Dutch East India Company had had a monopoly on the spice trade. Rumpf attained wealth and esteem, and with great success dedicated himself, despite having been blinded on an excursion in 1669, to a scientific investigation of the island. Commissioned by Rumpf's publishers, Merian drew numerous marine invertebrates for the plate section of the *D'Amboinsche Rariteitkamer*, without however being mentioned in the Amsterdam printing of 1705.

Presumably, Merian was still only concerned with her own – and last – book, which was also published in Amsterdam in 1705: *Metamorphosis Insectorum Surinamensium. Ofte Verandering der Surinaamsche Insecten* ("The Meta-

morphosis of Surinam Insects. Frequent Transformation of the Surinam Insects"). This magnificent volume in imperial folio format represents the completion of her life's work. If the book of caterpillars in quarto format can be regarded as her primary scientific work, the large-format Surinam book is without doubt her supreme artistic achievement.

In the *Book of Flowers*, Merian eschewed picture commentaries entirely. In the book of caterpillars, the commentaries occupy twice as many pages as the illustrations. In the Surinam book, she ultimately chose a happy medium. The sixty large plates are now completely dominant, while the explanatory texts, which are brief and concise, are placed opposite. She depicts fruits (such as pineapples, pomegranates, bananas or melons) and trees (ranging from Indian jasmine to the rubber tree which she encountered in the 'Providentia' plantation of the governor's widow), as well as some flowers (lilies, roses, etc.). As in the book of caterpillars, Merian's prime concern in this, her third work, is not with the plants, but, again, with a fascination for metamorphosis in the world of butterflies and other insects. She writes in the preface that she shows, in the ninety observations of caterpillars, worms and maggots, how these change colour and form upon shedding their skin, and ultimately turn into butterflies, noctuid moths, beetles, bees and flies. She places all these animals on the plants, flowers and fruits on which they subsist. Additionally, she depicts spiders, ants, snakes, lizards, toads and frogs, mostly on the basis of her own observations, and some according to the descriptions of the native inhabitants.

The Surinam book represents a highlight of early eighteenth-century European book art. For Merian, it was a great risk, from both a financial and physical point of view. Her hopes of reaching a wider public in England and Germany and thus of being able to finance the costly expedition were dashed; only small editions, in Latin and Dutch respectively, could be printed. In the accompanying volume to the Dresden facsimile of the Surinam book, Helmut Deckert mentioned fourteen copies in twelve public libraries. Nine are coloured, six of these possibly by Maria Sibylla Merian herself (Basle, Dresden, Frankfurt am Main, Jena, Nuremberg and Vienna). It is not known how many copies in total she printed, sold or coloured herself. All the more revealing are contemporary travel reports, such as that of the Frankfurt scholar

Zacharias Conrad von Uffenbach, who visited Merian in Amsterdam in 1711. He bought "several originals" and several signed book editions, including for forty-five guilders a hand-coloured copy of the Surinam book.

The Russian Tsar, Peter the Great, had also toured Holland in 1716 and 1717, in order to acquire treasures for his art collection at auctions, galleries and from collections of rare objects. While on his travels, he was advised by the still-life painter and art dealer Georg Gsell (1673-1740) of St. Gallen, who lived in Amsterdam and who was married (his third marriage) to Dorothea Maria Merian (1648-1743), Maria Sibylla's younger daughter. Hence, the Tsar became acquainted with Merian's works first-hand, and instructed his physician in ordinary, Dr. Robert von Areskin, to acquire a two-volume collection of her paintings on parchment for 3,000 Dutch guilders. It was quite by chance that on this day, January 13, 1717, the day of the written purchase agreement, Maria Sibylla Merian died.

After the Tsar's death, the colourful illustrations came into the property of the Academy of Sciences in St. Petersburg.[20] Presumably, Areskin had acquired Merian's study book for himself, which with his death in 1718, also came into the Tsar's property and later ended up in the library at the same academy.[21]

The Gsells, incidentally, accepted the Tsar's invitation to St. Petersburg, where the artist was appointed court painter and custodian of the painting gallery, while his wife oversaw the collection of rare objects. Both gave drawing lessons at the Academy, established in 1725, using Merian's studies as display material. Later, her son-in-law, Leonhard Euler, recalled in his autobiography that Dorothea Maria Gsell, like her mother Maria Sibylla, mainly painted flowers and insects. In 1736, Dorothea Maria and Georg Gsell sold many of Maria Sibylla's watercolours to the St. Peters-

burg Academy. The inheritance of the elder daughter, Johanna Helena, was kept in the Royal Library in Windsor Castle in 1755, after having been bought at auction by George III, and in 1759 it came into the ownership of the British Museum, via the collection of Sir John Sloane (1660-1753).

Nine editions of Maria Sibylla Merian's three works were published during her lifetime, between 1675 and 1717. With the dissolution of her estate and the Gsells' departure for St. Petersburg, the heirs sold all the copperplate engravings to the publisher Johannes Oosterwijk. Thereafter – between 1718 and 1771 – a total of ten further posthumous editions of the book of caterpillars and the Surinam book were published in Latin, Dutch and French, in Amsterdam, The Hague and Paris.

The *Book of Flowers* was reissued in 1730, in a greatly modified form. The publisher Frédéric Bernard had acquired the copper plates, had had them altered by another artist's additions, and published them in a *Histoire des Insectes de l'Europe*, together with other copperplate engravings. "He printed them in threes or mostly in fours on a folio page, and hence robbed the individual pages of their intimacy."[22]

Like the house in which Merian was born, and her grave, the copper plates, too, seem to have disappeared. We have access to her through her artistic work, preserved in museums, libraries and archives, and made accessible by facsimiles. Meanwhile, the memory of the natural scientist and publisher has been kept alive in public life in many different ways. These include a German postage stamp with her portrait issued in 1987 and, in 1992, a banknote for five hundred German marks. In the jubilee year of 1997, her native town of Frankfurt am Main dedicated a large memorial exhibition to her, with a catalogue to summarize the current state of research.

The *Book of Flowers* is the artist's first work, and is of great rarity. Merian published it in three volumes, each with twelve plates. The first volume, from 1675, originally had a Latin title page (*Florum Fasciculus Primus*); this version is only known on the basis of one copy in Bern. The second volume followed in 1677, and in 1680 the third, both with German title pages. With the publication of the third volume, Merian, meanwhile aged thirty-three, compiled a new edition comprising all three sections, and now called her work the *New Book of Flowers*. The purchaser could hence complete and bind together the already acquired first two sections with the third, the new preface and the register. Alternatively, from 1680 on, the completely new edition could be acquired.

Helmut Deckert has described six complete copies of the *New Book of Flowers* in Bern, Dresden, Leipzig, Mainz and South Kensington.[23] Of the three coloured copies formerly in Dresden, one was destroyed during wartime (in the former Botanisches Institut der Technischen Hochschule). The copy in the Sächsische Landesbibliothek – Staats- und Universitätsbibliothek zu Dresden is bound in a leather cover with a Palatinate elector's coat of arms. The provenance and the enchanting colouring indicate that Merian coloured it herself for the Palatinate elector. Presumably, this volume later came to the Dresdner Hofbibliothek as a gift, where it was first listed in a catalogue in 1749. The volume published here has been produced on the basis of this copy. The two missing illustrations of the basket of flowers and vase of flowers (Section 3, Plates 2 and 3), have been taken from the third copy of the Bibliothek des Landesamts für Denkmalpflege in Dresden, which in many cases features a coarser, markedly different colouring. Of all the copies described, only the one in Mainz is uncoloured. Additional, uncoloured pages have been preserved in Nuremberg and Vienna.

The way that these few books and individual pages have come down to us suggests that the three sections, with twelve plates each, had found practical use as pattern pages and as models for embroidery, needlework and painting, as Merian had encouraged in the preface. Hence, the *New Book of Flowers* is an example of "utility literature" or "utility graphic arts", which have been more rarely preserved in museums and libraries than those handed-down, non-utility objects already judged by contemporary observers as worthy of being collected. It is no wonder, then, that essentially only the elaborately coloured and – as representative of their owners – bound copies have come down to us. This applies all the more to the *New Book of Flowers*, since it had no claims to being scientific, and, with its thirty-six plates – compared with 150 for the three-part book of caterpillars and sixty for the Surinam book – is small in scope.

It is this formal, intermediate status between practical guide and artistic collection, and the search (in terms of content) for new forms of expression and representation, which, in addition to its great rarity, constitute the special appeal and value of this *New Book of Flowers*. According to the Nuremberg *Maler-Ordnung* 'Painters' Regulations') of 1596, women were not permitted to paint professionally. By contrast, working with fabrics was deemed appropriate for women. Sewing and embroidery were considered "fine science for the women's room". Hence, in 1700, Margaretha Helm published a Nuremberg *Neh- und Strickbuch* ('Sewing and Knitting Book') with more than fifty copper plates, in order to supply "such fine science of all kinds for the women's room … patterns and sketches in the newest style." Moreover, in 1676, the engraver Rosina Helena Fürst published a *Model Buch*, also in Nuremberg, in which she, too, emphasized the division of labour between the sexes: "Hence, the labour is equally divided, and there is much that is more suited to the male, more to the female [gender], hence, when the same is exchanged, and women's work is done by men, or men's work by women, one as well as the other will bring accusations, disgrace and dishonour, for the one who steps outside of the restrictions of his vocation."[24]

In the face of such restrictions on role and profession, Merian does not want to break any taboos, but rather work within the existing possibilities, and cautiously extend creative freedoms. Her standing with respect to Latin is revealing, the language in which scientific treatises, i.e., botanical books, were generally written in the seventeenth century. Merian had not learned Latin as a girl, which is why she later tried to teach herself the fundamentals. In keeping with the conventions of the time, her books open with a main title in Latin, but from the subtitle onwards continue in German (*New Book of Flowers*, book of caterpillars) or Dutch (Surinam book). The "omnibus" edition of the *New Book of Flowers* ultimately eschews Latin elements in the title, together with the associated pretensions. In the preface to the Surinam book, Merian does pay due respect to the botanists of the time, but she avoids giving her works a scholarly tone by including quotations from these authorities. This left her view clear for her own observations, not only in books, but also in nature. It is to these that we are indebted for the new findings with respect to metamorphosis.

This originality was, of course, a learning process, which had begun with a child's perspective and with books. Merian not only created a basis for others, but also took ideas and models from books herself. In 1612, her grandfather, Johann Theodor de Bry, had published a *Florilegium Novum*, a *New Blumbuch Darinnen allerhand schöne Blumen und frembde Gewächs* (a 'new book of flowers, containing all sorts of beautiful flowers and exotic plants'), in Latin and German. After impressive artistic and pleasure gardens had been established in the residences of the nobility and in the wealthy towns, this handbook, with its more than one hundred copperplates, was intended to lend wings to the new fashion and help to stock the gardens "with both exotic and indigenous plants." In 1641, her father published a new, expanded edition, this time completely in Latin and with a dedication to the Frankfurt senator Johannes Schwind, whose magnificent French gardens were also depicted. Some of Maria Sibylla's copperplate engravings of flowers are preserved in this *Florilegium*, but the differences in representation, in comparison with the *New Book of Flowers*, are much greater than the similarities. De Bry/Merian attempt to depict schematically as many varieties as possible, together with their Latin names; in the case of Maria Sibylla on her own, however, the accent is on the selection and its artistic, decorative reproduction. For this reason, she did not engrave the Latin plant names into the copperplates. She lists the plant names only in the register, and only in German.

The influences from Nicolas Robert's (1614-1685) floral atlas, which Max Anton Pfeiffer described in 1936, are more obvious. Robert was a French court painter from 1644 onwards, and was highly regarded for his naturalistic representations of plants and animals. He published books of flowers in Rome and Paris, and painted on parchment for Ludwig XIV.

Merian adopted seven motifs from his atlas *Variae ac Multiformes Florum species*, printed in Rome in 1665, reproduced either the right way round or reversed, in the first section of her *Book of Flowers*. Moreover, the flower garlands of the second and third sections are orientated towards his *Plusieurs Guirlandes, vases et bouquets des fleurs*, published in 1673.

Taking her adoption of the daffodils (I, 4) and the Bearded Iris (I, 8) as examples, it becomes clear that Merian varied the originals in a revealing manner.[25] In the case of the daffodils, Merian shifted the butterfly to the left-hand side, in order to make room on the right for a caterpillar. In the case of the Bearded Iris, she placed a butterfly on the left-hand side, in so doing sacrificing a leaf. It is these adapted copies which show the artist's emphasis on design, and her approach to breathe artistic life into floral pictures.

With the pattern and model pages of her *New Book of Flowers*, Merian wanted to encourage others to imitate her example or copy her work. Hence, she was not afraid to borrow from different sources herself. With an increase in interest in nature studies since the Renaissance, artists searched for contemporary representation of plants and animals. Models were found in the work of Albrecht Dürer, or the court painter of the Medici, Jacopo Legozzi, noted for the exquisiteness of his floral representations. Of course, the orientation towards models meant that the original works or their reproductions had to be accessible.

The floral representations of Nicolas Robert, already mentioned above, were accessible in the form of technical reproductions, as were the representations of plants and animals by the Dutch painter of miniatures and court painter under Kaiser Rudolph II, Joris Hoefnagel (1542, Antwerp – 1601, Vienna). His son, Jacob Hoefnagel, published his *Archetypa studiaque Patris Georgii Hoefnagelii* in 1592, in Frankfurt, and his *Diversae Insectarum Volatilium Icones ad vivum* in 1630, in Amsterdam. For both publications, the son transferred his father's watercolours of plants, fruits and insects into forty-eight copperplates (*Archetypa*), and sixteen etchings with 302 representations of insects (*Insectarum Volatilium Icones*). In turn, Ulisse Aldrovandi (1522-1605), natural scientist and founder of the botanical gardens in Bologna, took his inspiration from the *Archetypa*. For his scientific treatises, Aldrovandi had more than 10,000 watercolours and woodcuts prepared by various artists, including Ligozzi. Besides Conrad

Gessner, Aldrovandi was one of the first systematic collectors of insects, and his folio volume, *De Animalibus Insectis*, first published in 1602, was the entomological standard work of the seventeenth century. Merian drew inspiration from all these books for her own work, which, in turn, inspired the Nuremberg books of flowers and insects in the early eighteenth century.

In the fine arts, as in literature, imitation and creation represented a dynamic process, in the course of which accusations of plagiarism played a greater role only in more recent times. Literary compilation or the copying of pictures fell out of favour when these activities fostered outdated points of view and hindered insights, or when reproductions became widespread and degenerated in a commercial sense. By contrast, imitating and copying good and new sources was seen in a positive light, since – through the impacts of war – culturally "belated" Germany was directly dependent on the impetus of neighbouring countries. Owing to the artistic proximity of the model and its adaptation, it is often difficult to distinguish between an original and a copy, both in art and in literature.

Merian tried to present her floral pictures in a decorative and varied manner. She depicted twenty plants on their own: seven flowers growing out of the ground or appearing to be inserted into it, while one illustration in each of the three sections depicts a small floral bouquet tied up with a bow. Single flowers dominate in both of the first two sections, while the third section is dominated by arrangements of at least three flowers each. She enlivens these floral studies by including twenty-seven butterflies, beetles, spiders and insects. It is striking that these are not evenly distributed throughout the book: in the first section, she depicts seventeen small animals, while not depicting any at all in fifteen illustrations of the last two sections. It is possible that they were not supposed to detract from the impact of these artificial arrangements. Did Merian, in view of her work on her book of caterpillars, want to restrict the function of the final two sections of the *Book of Flowers* to that of models for floral painting and embroidery? An interesting tension and diversity arises regardless, owing to the differences mentioned above. These are further enhanced by the vase and basket of flowers, as well as by the garlands.

The floral still life on the Chinese vase looks like a watercolour on parchment: "The flowers are placed next to one another, without overlapping; as a result,

spatial depth is not produced. The principle is equivalent to the flat, radial compositions of Dutch floral still-life painting at the end of the sixteenth and beginning of the seventeenth century."[26]

Merian assembles the best-known and most popular plants of the time in the *New Book of Flowers*. She depicts individual hyacinths, narcissi, tulips, anemones, an iris, a Turk's cap lily, pansies, a rose, and peonies in the first section. Auricles, a crown imperial, a tulip, wallflowers, a buttercup, an iris, and carnations follow in the second section.

The tulip, which originated from Persia, and which was introduced into Europe in 1550, stirred up feelings throughout Europe. In the preface, Merian describes the excesses of the "tulip mania" of the 1630s, when 2,000 Dutch guilders were paid for a single 'Semper Augustus', and as much as 70,000 guilders offered for a tulip garden. Other sources mention more than 10,000 guilders in connection with new varieties. The excesses of the tulip trade led to speculation and ultimately, in 1637, to the collapse of the market. The much older crown imperial originated from the western Himalayas or from Iran, and was widely distributed throughout Europe from the Middle Ages onwards. Its early popularity is evident from illustrations in manuscripts of the Middle Ages and the early Modern age. Like many of the flowers, Merian also painted the crown imperial on more than one occasion. In the 'Leningrader Aquarellen' (Plate I, 6), it is depicted not with a pinkish-red flower, but with a vivid yellow one.

A complete register of works would make it possible to demonstrate the numerous parallels, similarities, and further developments among Merian's studies, watercolours and copperplate engravings. In her study book, for example, she drew hyacinths or anemones that she adopted in later representations, an indication of the method and economy of her work.

Some plants in the *New Book of Flowers*, such as the tulip, hyacinth, rose, lily, iris or carnation, are also found in a modified form in the book of caterpillars. As with the larkspur in the study book, caterpillars, pupae and butterflies appear to be placed on the feed plants so that they are easily recognizable and hence attract attention in preference to the flower. Merian explained her intentions and procedure in the preface to the book of caterpillars in 1679 as follows: "Hence, I choose to adorn my floral paintings with caterpillars/

butterflies/ and such small animals at any time; just as the landscape painters do with their pictures/ to make one just as alive with the other; hence, I have often made great efforts to capture these/ until/ by way of the silkworms/ I finally came to the transformation of the caterpillars/ and thought about the same/ whether or not there, too, a similar transformation takes place?"[27]

This concentration on depicting natural processes is what distinguishes Merian's painting from the widespread, emblematic, symbolic arts of her time. Emblems are structured in tripartite form with motto, picture and picture commentary, and show the intellectual and spiritual meaning in, and within, the objects. Occasionally, Merian turns to this art form herself, for example in the album page for her poet friend, Christoph Arnold. She painted a rose for him under the title 'Deß Menschen leben ist gleich einer Blum' (The life of a human is like that of a flower).[28]

The beauty of the flower and its transitory nature represented one of the most popular motifs in allegorical interpretations of the world, and the floral still life was perhaps the most colourful and most artistic expression of this central notion. The marvellous floral still lifes by Jacob Marrell and Abraham Mignon – some of which Merian had seen first-hand – also did not fail to give indications, either self-evident or hidden, of the transitory nature of this splendour. For example, Mignon (1640-1679), a very active still-life virtuoso in Frankfurt, Antwerp, and Utrecht, painted a bouquet of flowers with thistles, on which all sorts of small creatures such as snails, flies or beetles are depicted consuming the floral riches.

This natural process of decay (in a figurative sense) interested Merian less as a theological *memento mori* than as a biological stage of development. Her achievement lies in suppressing the widespread joy of interpretation in favour of simple (empirical) observation and description. Just how laden with meaning the world of flowers in the seventeenth century was, is shown – again, here only by way of example – by the literary unions of the time. In 1617, the Fruchtbringende Gesellschaft ('Productive Society') was founded to promote the German native language after the model of the Accademia della Crusca. Matthäus Merian the Elder printed the 'Book of the Society',[29] in which the symbolic image of a plant, with a corresponding interpretation, was assigned to each and every member.

Later, the Nuremberg patrician and senator Georg Phillipp Harsdörffer founded the Pegnesischer Blumenorden in 1644, a floral order whose members pursued the high art of linguistic floral metaphors in poems and pictures.

The Hamburg poet and senator Barthold Hinrich Brockes (1680-1747) paved the way for a shift in literary orientation away from the level of the symbolic picture towards that of real objects with his cycle of poems, *Irdisches Vergnügen in Gott* ('Earthly delight in God', 1721-1747). With exact, detailed descriptions, Brockes wanted to open the eyes of his readers so that they could recognize the beauties of nature and, with this realization, participate in a 'rational and comprehensible divine service':

Open, O open your eyes and see,
How glorified everything is in the spring,
    How lovely do bloom the gardens in splendour!
    Open your lips, come, praise and extol
The wonders of the Creator, by whom alone
Field, forests, and gardens are glorified![30]

According to him, the beauty of creation can and should be clear to – and can be experienced by – everyone in every small creature. In view of such joy of realization, the transitions from contemplation to observation, from pious interpretation to exact perception, are fluid. To praise God in the diverse phenomena of nature also means to take the reality of the world seriously, to come to know it, and hence to enhance its status. This process of revaluation already seems to be apparent in Merian's pictures of forty years earlier.

In his *Irdisches Vergnügen in Gott*, Brockes describes in hundreds of poems the beauties of nature, the elements, sky, animals, and also flowers and insects. Some poems can, as it were, be read as a commentary to Merian's pictures – for example the verses on the garden, rose, crown imperial, grape-hyacinth, frogs or beetles. These instructive verses were still written entirely in the symbolic spirit of the Baroque:

The bitter-sweet scent,
That springs from the crown imperials,
Is also a picture filled with instruction
That even the highest state
Is oft filled with bitterness.[31]

Brockes' scientific, aesthetic sense is directed towards the microscopically small, but he does not forget to interpret what is seen and described in a Christian manner, entirely in the spirit of physicotheology. With some disgust, the poet describes the life of a dung beetle in horse manure, finally interpreting in a moral sense its ability to crawl out of the dung into the fresh air. Merian shared Brockes' reservations with respect to depicting the 'no longer beautiful', but, as a natural scientist, she was unafraid of painting natural objects and naming them by their name, certainly not in an 'unbeautified' manner, but instead artistically stylized in her own way.

A century after Merian's death, Goethe, in his contemplation of floral painting,[32] recalled the fruitful ambivalence of Merian's works "between art and science, between the inspection of nature and the aims of painting". With the division of art and science into separate disciplines, and with the development of their specializations since the nineteenth century, it has become more difficult to evaluate and appreciate her work by contemporary and modern standards. For with the modern differentiation and estrangement of the disciplines, our admiration increases for all those multitalented artists – from da Vinci to Goethe – who united arts and sciences in their life's work, and who were able to make them mutually productive.

Merian's greatness lies in the constant movement between the scientific observation of nature and artistic practice, and in her ability to convey one with, and by means of, the other. Hence, any one-sided criticism from an artistic or scientific point of view is inadequate. She studied the world of the flowers and small creatures with perseverance and rigour, from her youth until old age, and implemented her knowledge in an artistic manner as a freelance painter and copperplate engraver. With her watercolour and graphically reproduced scientific illustrations she was able to hold her ground in Protestant Germany's overly saturated artistic market.

Subsequent generations have taken up this impressive achievement in several ways. Biologists and entomologists named plants and animals that she had described after her, while later artists imitated her style. For historical research on women, Merian's life and work are interesting starting points for delineating the conditions and possibilities for her personality to develop against the background of her gender and family history.

For Merian herself, it must have been satisfying to be able to stand alongside Matthäus the Elder, her renowned father. His city views and her pictures of flowers and insects are an expression of their *savoir faire*, their creative lives, and artistic precision. Above all, they are testimonies of their time that have remained alive and vivid to this day. The children's books on Maria Sibylla Merian are an eloquent testimony of this vividness. They show that not only art and science, but also dream and reality touched the life of this woman.

93

1. Joséphine Le Foll has traced the history of floral painting from the antiquity to the present day (*La peinture des fleurs*, 1997), and in so doing has devoted much space to the rich floral bouquets of the Baroque and to the magnificent gardens of the Impressionists. Unfortunately, there is no reference whatsoever to Maria Sibylla Merian's imposing life's work, although it was this artist in particular who had contributed "with her interest in insects and the culture of caterpillars to breathing new artistic life into the floral piece", as Sybille Ebert-Schifferer emphasizes in her excellent *Geschichte des Stillebens* (1998).

2. So muß Kunst und Natur stets mit einander ringen/
bis daß sie beederseits sich selbsten so bezwingen/
   damit der Sieg besteh' auf gleichen Strich und Streich:
   Die überwunden wird/ die überwindt zugleich!

3. A French term meaning optical illusion, a popular method of simulating real three-dimensionality in paintings, especially in the Baroque.

4. Cf. p. 86.

5. Pfister-Burkhalter, p.11.

6. Ibid., p. 12.

7. Leningrader Studienbuch, 2, p. 141.

8. "Johann Andreas Graf/ Mahler/ verheuratet sich an Maria Sibilla Merianin, zierliche Mahlerin in Blumen: Nehet auch mit der Nadel gar natürliche und lebhafte Blumen: Etzet solche." Sandrart: *Teutsche Academie*, 2, p. 339.

9. Ibid.

10. Ibid.

11. "Johann Andreas Graf von Nürnberg ... verheuratete sich zu Frankfurt mit des berühmten M. Merian Kupferstechers Tochter/ Namens Maria Sibilla Merianin, als die von Stamm ab/ und eigner Begierde zu der edlen Mahlerey inclinierte/ wie sie dann/ vermittel dieses Heuraths/ die verlangte gute Information in der Zeichen-Kunst und Mahlen mit Oel und Waßerfarben auf allerley Zieraht in Blumen/ Früchten und Geflügel/ besonderlich auch in den Excrementen der Würmlein/ Fliegen/ Mucken/ Spinnen und dergleichen Natur der Thieren auszubilden/ mit samt dern Veränderungen/ wie selbige Anfangs seyn/ und hernacher zu lebendigen Thieren werden/ samt dern Kräutern/ wovon sie ihre Nahrung haben/ mit großen Fleiß/ Zier und Geist/ so wol in der Zeichnung/ als in den colorirten Farben/ und Rundirungen meisterhaft zuwegen gebracht/ besonderlich mit einer Art von Waßerfarben auf seidenen Tafeln/ Atlas oder andern Stoffen/ auch auf Leinwat mahlet sie allerhand zierliche Blumen und Kräuter/ und daß solche auf beeden Seiten des Leinwats in gleicher Vollkommenheit erscheinen/ und welches an [sic] verwunderlichsten ist/ so mögen solche gemahlte Leinwaten ohne Gefahr der Farben wieder gewaschen werden ... dergleichen täglich aus ihren espedienten Händen zu Schein kommen/ daß sie dannenhero in dieser ruhmwürdigen Kunst/ der natürlichen Blumen/ Kräutern und Thieren/ allervollkommenst zu seyn das Lob hat; wie ingleichen mit Seiden alles oberzehltes wahrhaftig und natürlich durch die Nadel zu bilden/ höchstberühmt ist/ wie sie dann zu mehrerer Beyhülf denen/ die solche Tugenden zu lernen und zu folgen verlangen/ dergleichen curiose Lectionen gezeichnet/ und in Kupfer sauber und vernünftig gesetzt hat ..."

12. *Der Raupen wunderbare Verwandelung/ und sonderbare Blumen-nahrung/ worinnen/ durch eine gantz-neue Erfindung/ Der Raupen/ Würmer/ Sommer-vögelein/ Motten/ Fliegen/ und anderer dergleichen Thierlein/ Ursprung/ Speisen/ und Veränderungen/ samt ihrer Zeit/ Ort und Eigenschaften/ Den Naturkündigern/ Kunstmahlern/ und Gartenliebhabern zu Dienst/ fleissig untersucht/ kürtzlich beschrieben/ nach dem Leben abgemahlt/ ins Kupfer gestochen/ und selbst verlegt ...*

13. Es ist Verwunderns werth/ daß ihnen auch die Frauen
       dasjenige getrauen
         zu schreiben/ mit Bedacht/
     was der Gelehrten Schaar so viel zu thun gemacht.
     Was Gesner/ Wotton/ Penn/ und Mufet überlassen/
       in Schriften zu verfassen;
         das hat dir/ Engelland/
     mein Teutschland nachgethan/ durch kluge Frauenhand.

14. "Suche demnach hierinnen nicht meine/ sondern allein Gottes Ehre/ Ihn/ als einen Schöpfer auch dieser kleinsten und geringsten Würmlein/ zu preisen ..."

15. "5.
    Schauet an die ringen Kräutlein/
       womit Er die Würmer speist;
    alle Blumen/ Zweig' und Stäudlein/
       da sie die Natur hinweist/
    müssen so viel tausend nehren/
    und uns GOTTES Vorsorg lehren:
       Schauet an die schlechte Weid'/
       Und ihr stolzes Purpurkleid.

    7.
    Liebster GOTT/ so wirst Du handeln
       Auch mit uns/ zu seiner Zeit;
    Wie die Raupen sich verwandeln/
       Die/ durch ihre Sterblichkeit/
    wiederum lebendig werden/
    gleich den Todten/ in der Erden;
       Laß mich armes Würmelein
       Dir alsdann befohlen seyn!"

16. "Sintemal ich sonst diß mühsame Werklein nie angefangen/ viel weniger in Druck zu geben mich überreden lassen: Absonderlich/ wann man mir solches/ als einer Frauen/ (die nur neben ihrer Haussorge diß zusamm tragen müssen) für eine unziemende Ehrsucht halten solte." Book of Caterpillars, 1, p. 102.

17. Der Anfang ist gemacht; wird dieses nun belieben/
Sor werd' ich micht forthin/ zu Dienst dem Leser/ üben/
   Daß ich ihn bey dem Lust erhalte/ durch die Kunst/
   Damit man Lob verdient/ und grosser Herren Gunst!

18. Pfister-Burkhalter, p. 38.

19. Letter to Clara Regina Imhoff, July 25, 1682, *Merian. Künstlerin und Naturforscherin*, p. 262.

20. Critically edited in 1974, as the *Leningrader Aquarelle*

21. Critically edited in 1976, as the *Leningrader Studienbuch*

22. Pfister-Burkhalter, p. 19.

23. Accompanying volume to the facsimile edition of 1966 (3rd edition, 1981).

24. *Merian. Künstlerin und Naturforscherin*, p. 96.

25. Illustration in Pfister-Burkhalter, pp. 16f.

26. *Merian. Künstlerin und Naturforscherin*, p. 118.

27. "Dieweil ich meine Blumen-mahlerey mit Raupen/ Sommer-

vögelein/ und dergleichen Thierlein auszuzieren/ mich jederzeit befliessen; dergleichen die Landschaft-Mahler mit ihren Bildern thun/ eines durch das ander gleichsam lebendig zu machen: Also hab ich oft grosse Mühe in Auffangung derjenigen angewandt/ bis ich endlich/ vermittelst der Seidenwürmer/ auf der Raupen Veränderung gekommen/ und denselben nachgedacht/ ob nicht dort auch eben dergleichen Verwandelung vorgehen möchte?"

28. *Merian. Künstlerin und Naturforscherin*, illustration p. 88.

29. Der Fruchtbringenden Gesellschaft Vorhaben, Nahmen, Gemaelde und Wörter, Frankfurt am Main: Merian, 1646.

30. Eröffnet, ach öffnet die Augen, und seht,
    Wie alles im Frühling verherrlichet steht,
        Wie lieblich die gläntzenden Gärten beblühmet!
    Eröffnet die Lippen, kommt, preiset und rühmet
    Die Wunder des Schöpfers, durch welchen allein
    Feld, Wälder und Gärten verherrlichet seyn!
    Brockes, p. 88.

31. Der bitter-süßliche Geruch,
    So aus den Kaiser-Kronen quillt,
    Ist mit ein Lehr' erfülltes Bild
    Das auch der allerhöchste Stand
    Mit Bitterkeit oft angefüllt.
    Brockes, p. 60.

32. Johann Wolfgang von Goethe: *Über Kunst und Alterthum*, 1817. In: *Sämtliche Werke*, Artemis Gedenkausgabe, vol. 13, p. 782.

SELECTED BIBLIOGRAPHY

BROCKES, Bartold Hinrich: *Auszug der vornehmsten Gedichte aus dem Irdischen Vergnügen in Gott*. Facsimile of 1738 edition. Stuttgart, 1965.

DAVIS, Natalie Zemon: *Drei Frauenleben. Glikl. Marie de l'Incarnation. Maria Sibylla Merian*. Translated from English into German by Wolfgang Kaiser. Berlin, 1996.

DECKERT, Helmut: *Maria Sibylla Merians 'Neues Blumenbuch' (Nuremberg 1680)*. Accompanying text to the facsimile edition, after the copy in the Sächsische Landesbibliothek zu Dresden. Leipzig, 1966.

EBERT-SCHIFFERER, Sybille: *Die Geschichte des Stillebens*. Munich, 1998.

KAISER, Helmut: *Maria Sibylla Merian. Eine Biographie*. Düsseldorf and Zurich, 1997.

LE FOLL, Joséphine: *La peinture des fleurs*. Munich, 1997.

LUDWIG, Heidrun: "Von der Betrachtung zur Beobachtung. Die künstlerische Entwicklung der Blumen- und Insektenmalerin Maria Sibylla Merian in Nürnberg (1670-1682)". In: *Der Franken Rom. Nürnbergs Blütezeit in der zweiten Hälfte des 17. Jahrhunderts*. John Roger Paas, ed. Wiesbaden, 1995.

Matthäus MERIAN d.Ä. Exhib. cat. in Frankfurt am Main and Basle. (Ute Schneider, ed.) Frankfurt am Main, 1993.

Maria Sibylla Merian: Künstlerin und Naturforscherin. Kurt Wettengl, ed. Historisches Museum Frankfurt am Main. Ostfildern, 1997.

PFEIFFER, Max Anton: "Das 'Neue Blumenbuch' der Maria Sibylla Merian." In: *Philobiblon* 9 (1936).

PFISTER-BURKHALTER, Margarete: *Maria Sibylla Merian. Leben und Werk 1647-1717*. Basel, 1980.

RÜCKER, Elisabeth: *Maria Sibylla Merian 1647-1717. Ihr Wirken in Deutschland und Holland*. Bonn, 1980. (*Nachbarn*, 24, edited by the Kgl. Niederländischen Botschaft. With colour illustrations and bibliography.)

SANDRART, Joachim von: *L'Academia Todesca ... oder Teutsche Academie der Edlen Bau-, Bild und Mahlerey-Künste*. Nuremberg and Frankfurt am Main, 1675.

SEGAL, Sam: "Maria Sibylla Merian als Blumenmalerin". In: *Merian. Künstlerin und Naturforscherin*. Exhib. cat. Frankfurt am Main, 1997.

FACSIMILE EDITIONS

MERIAN, Maria Sibylla: *Neues Blumenbuch, Nürnberg 1680*. After the copy in the Sächsische Landesbibliothek zu Dresden. Accompanying text by Deckert Helmut. 2 volumes, Leipzig, 1966, 3rd edition 1981.

MERIAN, Marian Sibylla: *Leningrader Aquarelle*. Ernst Ullmann, ed., with collaboration of Helga Ullmann, Wolf-Dietrich Beer, Boris von Lukin. 2 volumes. Leipzig, 1974.

MERIAN, Maria Sibylla: *Metamorphosis Insectorum Surinamensium, Amsterdam 1705*. After the copy in the Sächsische Landesbibliothek zu Dresden. Accompanying text to the facsimile edition by Helmut Deckert. Transcription of the Dutch original text by Gerhard Worgt. 2 volumes. Leipzig, 1975.

MERIAN, Maria Sibylla: *Schmetterlinge, Käfer und andere Insekten. Leningrader Studienbuch*. Wolf-Dietrich Beer and Gerrit Friese, eds. Text: German, English, French, Russian. 2 volumes. Leipzig, 1976.

MERIAN, Maria Sibylla: *Metamorphosis Insectorum Surinamensium*. Facsimile edition (of the Latin edition, Amsterdam 1705), after the watercolours in the Royal Library, Windsor Castle. 2 volumes. Elisabeth Rücker and William T. Stearn, eds., London 1982 (with extensive bibliography).

LIST OF FLOWER NAMES

The number given after each entry corresponds to the original numbering used by Maria Sibylla Merian on the flower pictures in the three sections of her original book. Plain numbers refer to the first section, numbers followed by a + to the second, and those followed by a - to the third.

Anemone (Anemone, Anemone)   7; 12+; 6-

Bearded Iris (Iris germanica L., blaue Lilie)   8

Bellflower (Campanula spec., blaues Wiesenglöcklein)   9-

Blue Passion-flower (Passiflora caerulea L., Passionsblume)   11-

Bluebell (Hyacinthoides/Scilla, blaue Sternhyazinthe)   5-

Caper (Capparis spinosa L., grosse Kapern-Blüte)   10-

Clove Pink or Carnation (Dianthus caryophyllus L., Negelein (Nelke) or Grasblumen-Stengel)   10+

Crocus (Crocus, Krokus)   7

Crown Imperial (Fritillaria imperialis L., einfache goldgelbe Kaiserkrone)   4+

Daffodil (Narcissus spec., Josephstab)   7

Daffodil, Bunch-flowered (Narcissus tazetta L., große orientalische Narzisse or Tazette)   2; 5

Daffodil, Common (Narcissus pseudonarcissus L., einfache Narzisse)   4

Dog's Tooth Violet (Erythronium dens-canis L., weisser Hundszahn)   4-

Dwarf Morning Glory (Convolvulus tricolor L., blauer Bindling)   8+

Forget-me-not (Myosotis spec., Vergißmeinnicht)   12-

Fritillary (Fritillaria, Fritillari)   7

Fritillary, Double (Fritillaria spec., gefüllte Fritillarien)   5-

Garden Auricula (Gartenaurikel; Primula x pubescens Jacq., Schlüsselblume)   3+

Garden Pansy (Viola x wittrockiana Gams, Gartenstiefmütterchen)   10

Garden Poppy (Mohn, Papaver somniferum L., Magsamen-Blume)   9-

Hyacinth, Common Garden (Hyacinthus orientalis L., Hyazinthe)   3; 4-

Hyacinth, Double (Hyacinthus spec., gefüllte Hyazinthe)   2

Hyacinth, Grape- (Muscari spec., Weintrauben-Hyazinthe)   4-

Iris (Iris, dunkelblaue Iris or Schwertlilie)   9+

Iris (Iris latifolia (Mil.) Voss, englische Iris)   7-

Iris, Persian (Iris persica L., Iris von Persien)   4-

Jasmine (Jasminum grandiflorum L., weisser Jasmin)   12+

Larkspur (Delphinium spec., gefüllter Rittersporn)   7-

Lily-of-the-Valley (Convallaria majalis L., Maiblümchen)   8-

Lily, Madonna (Lilium candidum L., weisse Lilie)   8+

Lily, Turk's Cap (Lilium pumilum DC., feinblättrige Lilie)   9

Marigold (Tagetes spec., Studentenblume)   12-

Nasturtium (Tropaeolum majus L., Kapuzinerkresse)   12-

Peony (Paeonia, Betonien-Rose)   12

Pheasant's Eye (Adonis annua L., Korallenblümlein)   8-

Pomegranate (Punica granatum L., Granaten-Blüte)   11+

Rose, Dutch (Rosa ›Hollandica‹, holländische Rose)   11

Rose, French (Rosa gallica L., Essigrose)   12+

Snowdrop (Galanthus nivalis L., Schneetröpflein)   8+

Spanish Broom (Spartium junceum L., Kunschrote)   10-

Squill, see Bluebell

Tuberose (Polianthes tuberosa L., Tuberosa)   8-

Tulip (Tulipa, Tulipane, Tulpe)   6; 5+; 5-

Turban (Persian) Buttercup (Ranunculus asiaticus L., feuerfarbene Ranunkel)   7+

Wallflower (Erysimum cheiri (L.) Crantz, grosser gelber Veil-Stengel, Goldlack)   6+